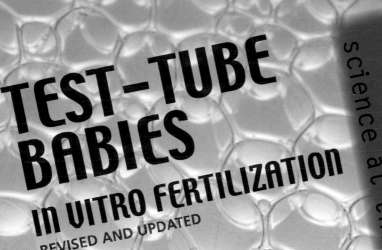

TEST-TUBE BABIES
IN VITRO FERTILIZATION
REVISED AND UPDATED

science at the edge

ANN FULLICK

Heinemann Library
Chicago, Illinois

© 2009 Heinemann Library
an imprint of Capstone Global Library, LLC
Chicago, Illinois

Customer service 888-454-2279

Visit our website at www.heinemannraintree.com

Printed and bound in China by South China Printing Company Ltd.

13 12 11 10 09
10 9 8 7 6 5 4 3 2 1

New edition ISBN: 978 1 4329 2453 9 (hardcover)

The Library of Congress has cataloged the first edition as follows:
Fullick, Ann, 1956-
      Test tube babies : in-vitro fertilization / Ann Fullick.
            p. cm. -- (Science at the edge)
Includes bibliographical references and index.
      ISBN 1-58810-703-5 (HC), 1-4034-4124-3 (Pbk.)
      I. Fertilization in vitro, Human--Juvenile literature. [I. Test tube babies. 2. Infertility. 3. Human reproduction.] I. Title. II. Series.
RG135 .F855 2002
618.1′78059--dc21
                                        2001006080

Acknowledgments
The author and publishers are grateful to the following for permission to reproduce copyright material:
© Associated Press p. **50**; © CARE at the Park p. **38**; © Corbis pp. **17** (Patrick Bennett), **41** (Bogdan Cristel/ Reuters), **49** (Cindy Yamanaka/Orange County Register), **53** (Scott T. Smith); © Doriver Lilley pp. **36**, **39**; © Getty Images pp. **43** (News), **23** (Popperfoto); © Mary Evans Picture Library p. **18**; © PA Photos pp. **32** (PA Archive/Andrew Parsons), **54** (AP Photo/Antonio Calanni), **57** (PA Archive/Andrew Parsons), **55**; © Photolibrary Group p. **30** (Digital Vision); © Photoshot p. **10** (Tetra Images); © Rex Features p. **22**; © Sally & Richard Greenhill p. **12**; © Science Photo Library pp. **4** (Stevie Grand), **7** (Prof. P. Motta/Dept. of anatomy/ University "La Sapienza", Rome), **9** (Bettina Salomon), **13**, **14**, **21** (Dr Yorgos Nikas), **25** (Mauro Fermariello), **26** (Living Art Enterprises, LLC), **27** (AJ Photo), **28** (Dr Yorgos Nikas), **42** (Hank Morgan), **45** and **48** (James King-Holmes); © Topham Picturepoint p. **43**.

Cover photograph of petri dish with eggs reproduced with permission of © Science Photo Library/ Mauro Fermariello.

CONTENTS

AN EVERYDAY MIRACLE?............4

WHAT CAUSES INFERTILITY?.........10

IS IVF THE ONLY WAY?..............16

THE IVF STORY 18

HOW DOES IVF WORK?..............24

THE PRICE OF SUCCESS..............32

DORIVER AND IAN'S STORY 36

BEYOND IVF......................40

ETHICS, ISSUES, AND THE LAW........48

WHERE DO WE GO FROM HERE?.......54

TIMELINE 58

GLOSSARY.......................60

FIND OUT MORE 63

INDEX 64

Some words are printed in bold, **like this**. You can find out what they mean by looking in the glossary.

AN EVERYDAY MIRACLE?

Every moment of every day a baby is born somewhere in the world. Each new human being comes into existence as the result of the joining of two tiny cells from the parents to form a single new cell. It is this cell that then grows and divides to form the billions of cells that make up the body of a newborn baby.

Although it happens every day, the arrival of a baby—which has grown over the course of nine months from a single, fertilized human egg cell—is an amazing event.

What Is Infertility?

For a lot of people, having babies is very easy. There is a time each month when, if a couple have sexual intercourse, there is a chance that an **ovum** (egg) in the body of the woman will be **fertilized** by a **sperm** from the man, and nine months later a baby will be born. Some people try to avoid pregnancy by using different methods of **contraception**, but what about when babies and pregnancy are wanted, yet do not happen?

The lives of many ordinary people have been impaired by the inability to have a much-wanted child. Although there are many different causes of **infertility**, for centuries the solutions were few and far between—adopting a child or becoming resigned to childlessness were the main options.

So what can people do about infertility today? In the last 50 years, it has become increasingly possible to treat and overcome at least some forms of infertility. A wide variety of options are now available to couples who cannot produce a child naturally. These range from simple tests that make it possible to pinpoint when a woman is most likely to get pregnant, to complex techniques, such as **in vitro** fertilization (IVF).

IVF is a form of treatment in which an egg and sperm are brought together outside the mother's body. They are usually mixed in a glass **petri dish**. This is how in vitro fertilization gets its name—*in vitro* is Latin for "in glass." The developing **embryo** is then replaced in the mother's body. The development of IVF has resulted in the births of thousands of babies around the world to people who would otherwise have had no hope of becoming pregnant.

IVF has led the way for the development of other methods to help couples have babies. These include injecting a single sperm into an egg before placing it back in the mother's body, and freezing embryos, eggs, and ovarian tissue that—when thawed—can produce healthy babies.

Like most scientific breakthroughs, our increased ability to control human **fertility** is something of a mixed blessing. It can bring great personal happiness to couples who would otherwise be unable to have their own child. At the same time it opens up many questions about embryos that are created and then not needed, and the possibility that inherited material of an embryo can be changed before it is returned to the mother.

As new and increasingly sophisticated treatments for infertility are discovered, the **ethics** of each method need to be discussed. Yet the driving force behind the whole technology of IVF remains the desperate desire of infertile couples to have a child of their own.

The Biology of Reproduction

Young children cannot have children of their own, but as we grow and mature, the parts of the body involved in making babies—technically known as **reproduction**—become active. These include the sexual organs and a gland in the brain. For many people these systems start up and run fairly smoothly, but for a growing number, things do not quite work as they should. So how does the body of a healthy, fertile woman or man work?

THE FERTILE FEMALE

For about two days in every month, a woman is fertile—she has produced an egg that is mature and ready to meet a sperm. The events leading up to and following this special time form a 28-day cycle of fertility, called the **menstrual cycle**.

Inside the body of every newborn baby girl are the eggs (called ova) that will form any children she may have in the future. Once the girl goes through **puberty**, the **ovaries**, which contain the eggs, become active in response to chemical signals called **hormones**.

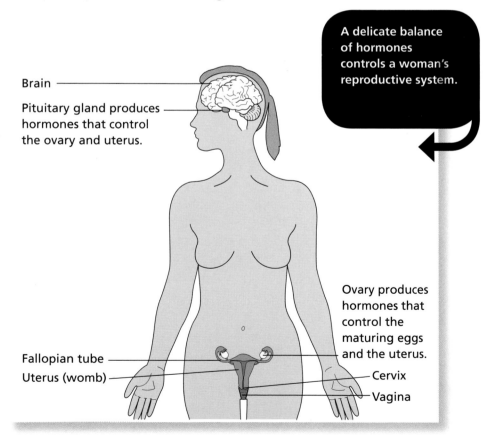

A delicate balance of hormones controls a woman's reproductive system.

Brain

Pituitary gland produces hormones that control the ovary and uterus.

Ovary produces hormones that control the maturing eggs and the uterus.

Fallopian tube

Uterus (womb)

Cervix

Vagina

Follicle Stimulating Hormone (FSH) is made by the **pituitary gland** in the brain, and it has a direct effect on the ovaries. It makes some of the eggs grow and mature, ready for release. FSH also makes the ovary produce another female hormone, **estrogen**. It triggers the buildup of the lining of the **uterus** (the organ in which a baby grows and develops) so it is ready to nurture a pregnancy. After about 14 days, an egg is released—this is known as **ovulation**—and it leaves the ovary. The egg travels through the **fallopian tube,** toward the uterus. If it meets sperm while on its way to the uterus, it may be fertilized, and a pregnancy begins. If not, the lining of the uterus gradually breaks down and passes out of the body. This is called menstruation.

REPRODUCTION IN THE MALE

Men do not have a reproductive cycle like women do, but they do have male reproductive hormones produced by the pituitary gland and by the male sex organs, the **testes**. In response to these hormones, the testes make a constant supply of sperm, and other glands make the various secretions that are mixed with the sperm to form **semen**.

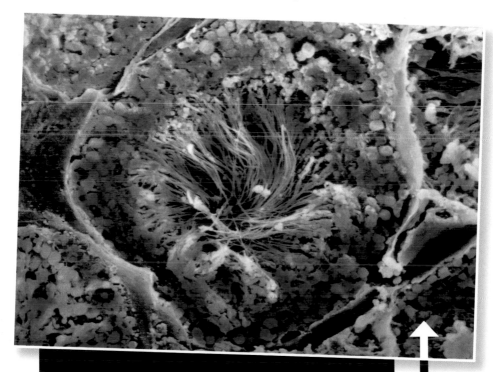

Whereas women usually produce a single, mature egg each month, millions of sperm are produced all the time in the testes. The tails of hundreds of developing sperm in the testes can be seen here.

From Conception to Birth

Once a couple decide that they are ready and want to have a baby, they need to try and make sure that sperm are present when a mature egg is released from the woman's ovary. Every time they have sexual intercourse, the man releases semen containing millions of sperm into the woman's vagina. At around the same time, if the woman is at the fertile point in her menstrual cycle, an egg will be released from the ovary and begin its journey along the fallopian tube. How do the egg and sperm meet?

The egg cannot move—it is pushed along the fallopian tube by the beating of millions of tiny hair-like cilia, which move it slowly away from the ovary toward the uterus. After ovulation, the egg only lives for around 48 hours.

The sperm, on the other hand, have an incredilby long journey to make. They travel through **mucus** and other secretions in the vagina and **cervix**, up through the uterus, and into the fallopian tube, which may contain the egg. The journey of a sperm is like a person swimming from the United States to the United Kingdom—through syrup!

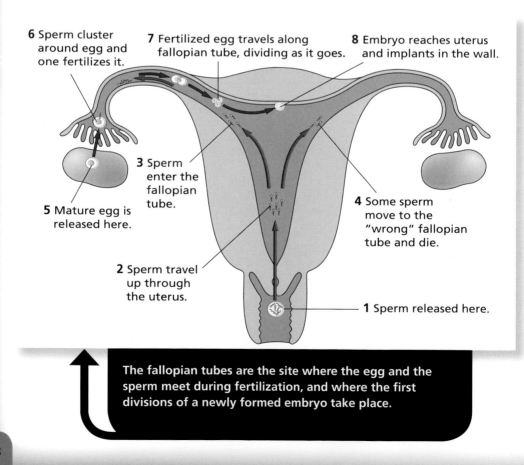

6 Sperm cluster around egg and one fertilizes it.

7 Fertilized egg travels along fallopian tube, dividing as it goes.

8 Embryo reaches uterus and implants in the wall.

3 Sperm enter the fallopian tube.

5 Mature egg is released here.

4 Some sperm move to the "wrong" fallopian tube and die.

2 Sperm travel up through the uterus.

1 Sperm released here.

The fallopian tubes are the site where the egg and the sperm meet during fertilization, and where the first divisions of a newly formed embryo take place.

Each sperm makes frantic lashing movements with its tail, which keep it suspended in the fluids, and it is moved to the egg by the natural muscle movement of the uterus. Some sperm reach the fallopian tubes very quickly—in a matter of minutes—but millions are lost along the way. This is why so many sperm are produced in the first place, because the odds against any of them reaching an egg are so high!

FERTILIZATION

Once sperm reach the egg, how is the egg actually fertilized? Sperm cluster around the egg, attracted by chemical messages it sends out. Special digestive **enzymes** in the head of the sperm act to dissolve away the protective jelly coating of the egg. Finally, a sperm breaks through and gets inside the egg—after that no other sperm can get in. The **nucleus** of the sperm contains **genetic** information from the man, while the nucleus of the egg contains genetic information from the woman. Once they fuse together, fertilization has taken place—a new genetic individual is formed, and a potential new life has begun!

After fertilization, the single cell begins to grow and divide while it continues to travel along the fallopian tube to the uterus. By the time it reaches the uterus, it is a small ball of cells ready to implant in the blood-rich lining that has developed in order to support it.

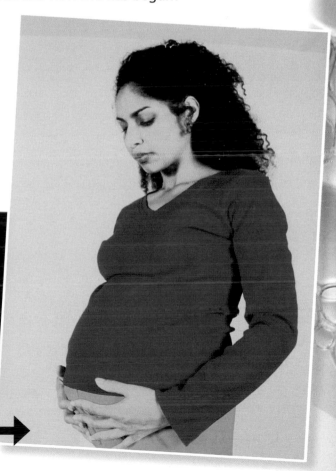

Once the fertilized egg has implanted in the uterus, cell divisions, the specialization of tissue, and development take place. After nine months, a fully formed baby human being is ready to emerge and take its place in the world.

WHAT CAUSES INFERTILITY?

When a couple decide that they want to start a family and begin to try to have a baby, they might expect to get pregnant right away. After all, many couples have spent years trying not to get pregnant. Even if a young, fertile couple have unprotected intercourse at the right stage of the monthly cycle, there is no guarantee that they will become pregnant. The probability that they will conceive gets steadily lower as they grow older, and it is also reduced by lifestyle factors such as smoking, drinking, and being overweight.

For an increasing number of couples, the months without a positive pregnancy test turn into years. When infertility seems to be staring people in the face, it becomes important to understand why pregnancy is not happening, and what, if anything, can be done about it.

When a wanted pregnancy does not happen, every monthly period can be a bitter disappointment.

Whose Problem?

It is almost inevitable that, if a couple cannot have a child, they wonder whose "fault" it is. For centuries, it was assumed that childlessness was the woman's fault. We now know better! Failing to get pregnant can be the result of problems in either partner or even both.

In about one-third of all cases of infertility, there is a problem in the way that the body of the woman is working. However, in more than one-third of cases, it is the reproductive system of the man that is not functioning as it should. The final group of infertility cases are either the result of both the man and the woman in a couple being less fertile than normal or, the most puzzling of all, both partners are theoretically healthy, but pregnancy just does not happen.

Finding Out

IVF has been successful in helping to overcome some forms of infertility, but it is still a highly specialized area of medicine. A couple who are having problems in conceiving a baby do not start their quest for a child with an IVF specialist—they begin with a family doctor.

Typically a doctor will check the general health of the couple in case there are any other causes of infertility not related to their reproductive systems. The doctor will check that the woman is not taking the contraceptive pill and determine whether the couple are having sexual intercourse at the time of the month when the woman is most fertile. The doctor will also check if either partner is taking any medications and whether either of them smoke or drink. Sometimes this allows the doctor to find a simple solution to fertility problems, so that medical intervention is not needed for the couple to start a family.

For many couples, the solution is not simple, and doctors will refer a couple to an infertility specialist when it becomes clear that they are having real difficulty in conceiving. For older couples, especially, the "biological clock" is ticking away fast, because a woman's fertility begins to fall as she approaches the age of 40. It is important that they start working with an infertility specialist as soon as possible. Most specialists would rather see couples with fertility problems sooner rather than later to try to find a successful solution to their problems.

An Infertile Woman ...

When a couple cannot conceive, a number of different tests are carried out on both partners to try and find out the cause of the infertility, because different causes need different solutions.

OVULATION PROBLEMS

To find out why a woman is not conceiving, doctors look for both physical and chemical causes. One of the first checks will be to see if ovulation is occurring, because no egg equals no baby.

By measuring the levels of different hormones in the blood, doctors can build up a reasonably good picture of what is going on and whether ovulation is taking place.

There can be several explanations for a lack of ovulation. Sometimes the situation is bleak—there are no eggs in the ovaries. However, this is relatively rare and is the cause of infertility in only one to two percent of women who have difficulty in conceiving. If there are no eggs, then the woman will never conceive naturally. IVF can help give her a chance at motherhood.

"Failure to ovulate is the cause of infertility in about three in ten cases. In some women this is a permanent problem. In some women it is intermittent when some months ovulation occurs and some months it doesn't."

Private Healthcare UK – website advising infertile couples about the causes of infertility

Some women who have had families of their own are prepared to act as egg donors. This means they allow eggs to be collected from their ovaries and given to other, infertile women. A donated egg can be fertilized by sperm from the man and placed in the infertile woman's body to develop.

For many women who do not ovulate, the problem is easier to fix. Some women do not make enough FSH to stimulate the release of mature eggs from the ovary, and others do not make any FSH at all. Synthetic (laboratory-created) hormones can be used that replace natural FSH, bringing about ovulation, and, hopefully, pregnancy (see pages 16–17).

TANGLED TUBES?

The most common physical problem preventing pregnancy in women is that the fallopian tubes are twisted, scarred, or blocked in some way. The fallopian tubes are located inside the body. They are about 11 centimeters (4 inches) long and lead from the ovaries to the uterus. If the tubes are damaged, the sperm can be prevented from meeting the egg, and even more importantly, can stop the egg, fertilized or not, from traveling to the uterus. Thirty percent of female infertility is the result of damaged fallopian tubes.

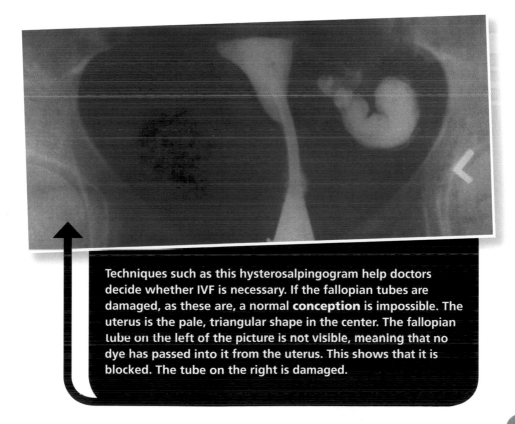

Techniques such as this hysterosalpingogram help doctors decide whether IVF is necessary. If the fallopian tubes are damaged, as these are, a normal **conception** is impossible. The uterus is the pale, triangular shape in the center. The fallopian tube on the left of the picture is not visible, meaning that no dye has passed into it from the uterus. This shows that it is blocked. The tube on the right is damaged.

Damage to the fallopian tubes is revealed during an investigation known as a **laparoscopy**, which is usually combined with a dye test. These tests give a good idea of whether or not the fallopian tubes are blocked or if there are any abnormalities in the uterus itself. If there appear to be problems, the investigation can be taken further with a hysterosalpingogram. In this test, a special dye that shows up on X-rays is injected up into the cervix. The dye shows blockages in the fallopian tubes on the X-rays that are taken.

Sometimes doctors can perform a technique using tiny instruments to try to reopen the fallopian tubes, but the technique itself can damage the delicate tubes. When the fallopian tubes are badly damaged or blocked, then the only hope of getting pregnant is IVF.

... Or an Infertile Man

When a couple visit their doctor about fertility problems, investigations will be made into the fertility of the man as well as the woman. There are two crucial factors: Is the man producing sperm in his semen, and are they normal, healthy, and active? The answer to both questions comes from an examination of the man's semen.

In normal, healthy semen there will be hundreds of millions of sperm. The lowest number of sperm counted as normal is 20 million sperm per 1 cubic centimeter (0.06 cubic inches) of semen! Once the sperm count falls below this level, it begins to affect fertility—remember that only one of every 2,000 sperm will make it from the cervix to the fallopian tubes. If the sperm count is just below normal, there are certain things that the man can do to help increase the numbers. For example, if the testes get too warm, the level of sperm production falls, so cool showers or baths, baggy underwear, and loose clothing can help to increase sperm count. Smoking and drinking alcohol are known to lower sperm numbers, so reducing or stopping these habits can also help to increase sperm count. If the count is too low, more may need to be done.

Using a microscope to view a fresh sample of semen reveals just what state the sperm are in, and how many of them there are.

NUMBERS AREN'T EVERYTHING

Overall sperm count is important, but the ability of sperm to fertilize eggs successfully depends on more than numbers. The motility of the sperm is very important, too—in other words, how active are they and how well do they swim? For the man to be fertile, his sperm need to have actively lashing tails and around 50 percent of them must swim forward in straight lines, rather than around in circles.

Even if a man has a lot of active sperm, he still may not be fertile. It is also important that the semen does not contain too many abnormal sperm. Every man produces a certain number of sperm with two heads instead of one, with two tails, or with broken necks. But if the percentage of these abnormal sperm gets too high, then the chances of a successful pregnancy fall. Abnormal sperm do not produce abnormal babies—they simply do not fertilize an egg.

Overcoming male infertility is not easy. Until recently, the best hope was for the woman to be treated with healthy sperm given by an unknown donor, often mixed with some of her partner's sperm. However, some of the latest developments of IVF involve using a single normal sperm and injecting it into the woman's egg cell, which is then implanted in her uterus. This exciting new development is leading to potential treatment for almost all men with fertility problems, especially since the number of men who produce no healthy sperm at all is relatively small. It has even become possible to take immature sperm from the testes (which are incapable of fertilizing an egg on their own) and inject the head of a sperm into an egg.

DISCUSS | Should Fertility Treatment Be Used to Pass on Faulty Genes?

Until recently, men who are affected by the genetic condition cystic fibrosis could not father children. They lack the tube that carries sperm away from the testes. People with cystic fibrosis did not used to live long into adulthood, so this was not a problem. But improvements in treatment mean that many people with cystic fibrosis now live into their 40s, so having children becomes more of an issue. A combination of new techniques means that these problems can be overcome. A small number of men with cystic fibrosis have been able to father children by having immature sperm removed from their testes and injected into the egg of their partner. But they definitely will have passed on the faulty cystic fibrosis gene to their children, who will at the very least be carriers of the disease. For the individuals concerned, it is wonderful that they can have their own child. But is it a good thing for society as a whole?

IS IVF THE ONLY WAY?

The best known treatment for infertility is IVF. It is often in the news headlines, in part because of the many new treatments that have been developed from it. However, when a couple first have fertility problems, treatment will not always involve IVF.

One of the most common ways to treat fertility problems involves **fertility drugs**. These are not only remarkably successful in their own right, but have also paved the way for the development of IVF. One of the main reasons women fail to get pregnant is because they do not produce mature eggs. Fertility drugs are chemicals that work in different ways to stimulate a woman's body to produce and release a mature egg from the ovary.

DISCUSS — Lifestyle and Infertility

Some of the most common causes of infertility result from lifestyle choices. How much people eat and exercise has a big effect on their chances of a successful pregnancy. But weight isn't the only thing that can cause infertility.

Smokers are more likely to have problems getting pregnant than nonsmokers. Smoking seems to affect the ovaries, so women smokers are less likely to ovulate successfully. If they do get pregnant, they have a higher risk of miscarriage or of their baby having birth defects. Men who smoke are more likely to have abnormal sperm that cannot fertilize an ovum. Stopping smoking does not solve the problem immediately, but within about three months, the reproductive systems are about the same as in nonsmokers.

Drinking alcohol can also affect fertility. In women, heavy drinking can disrupt the menstrual cycle and even prevent ovulation. In men, it reduces the quality and number of sperm produced and can also leave a man unable to have an erection, which makes intercourse and conception difficult. In most cases doctors advise people to change their behavior by losing or gaining weight or stopping drinking or smoking as a first step in the treatment of infertility. If people cannot or will not change their lifestyle, should they be given medical treatment?

"Excess weight reduces your chances of getting pregnant and staying pregnant. Being too thin stops your body producing eggs—so gives you no chance of pregnancy at all."

Dr. Richard Howell, obstetrician and gynecologist with a special interest in fertility treatment

The most widely used drug is clomiphene citrate. This drug works by fooling the body into making extra FSH, which stimulates the production of eggs by the ovaries. When women do not make any of their own FSH, they can be given different drugs that contain human hormones. These stimulate the ovaries directly. Other fertility drugs can be used if mature eggs are not being released from the ovaries.

The use of fertility drugs has been successful in helping many infertile couples to have children, and it has been vital in the development of IVF. To carry out this technique, doctors need to harvest a number of eggs that they can fertilize outside the body. Even with fertile women, only one or two eggs mature enough each month to be released from the ovary. When doctors are working with IVF patients, fertility drugs are an important part of the process.

FOCUS Multiple Births

Fertility drugs have helped many infertile couples to have children, but when they were first developed they caused problems of their own. In the early days of fertility drugs, doctors were not always sure of the doses to use, and many of the women using drugs had multiple pregnancies—in other words, more than one egg was released and fertilized at the same time. Twins did not cause too many problems, but far more people than expected had triplets, quadruplets, or an even larger number of babies.

Multiple pregnancies can lead to certain problems. When a lot of babies develop in the same uterus, there is a much increased risk that labor will start early, because the uterus becomes severely overstretched. Very small babies born at this stage are likely to die or become brain damaged. Today, due to increased knowledge of the way fertility drugs work and close control of the dosage, multiple pregnancies can usually be avoided.

These sextuplets were six months old in this photo.

THE IVF STORY

For centuries people have tried to overcome infertility by whatever means they had available. Scientists and doctors have traveled a long and difficult path to reach the stage we are at today, with IVF and other treatments holding out the hope of conception to many who would otherwise be unable to conceive. Many aspects of human fertility had to be understood before it became possible to fertilize a human egg outside of a mother's body and return it to her uterus to grow into a full-term, healthy baby.

For many years people had little understanding of how human reproduction worked. For example, a long-held belief was that the man supplied the entire new baby in the head of his sperm (see left), and the woman simply acted as a "seedbed," providing the growing child with all that it needed until it was born. Until beliefs such as this were overturned by scientific knowledge, any attempts to overcome infertility were doomed to fail.

Exploring ways of treating infertility is not a new science. In the third century, Jewish thinkers were discussing whether it was possible for people to become pregnant by accidental **artificial insemination**. By the 14th century, Arabs were using artificial insemination in horse-breeding.

In 1777 an Italian priest began experimenting with artificial insemination in reptiles, and in 1785 there was a major breakthrough, when John Hunter, a Scottish surgeon, made his first attempts at human artificial insemination. As a result of Hunter's experiments, a child was born that same year.

Into the 20th Century

The 20th century saw many significant advances in the treatment of infertility. In the early years of the century, scientists in the United States, including Samuel Crowe, Harvey Cushing, and John Homans, began to unravel the complex chemical control of human fertility. They discovered, isolated, and identified the hormones made by the pituitary gland in the brain and by the ovaries and testes.

Toward the end of the 20th century, there was a great deal of controversy and debate about IVF and some of the other treatments that have developed from it. However, this sort of debate is nothing new. Assisting couples in having babies using artificial means has always raised strong feelings. There have always been people unhappy with what they saw as an unnatural interference with nature.

When reports of artificial insemination using sperm from a donor were published in the *British Medical Journal* in 1945, there was great debate in the British Parliament. At that time British researchers were the leaders in the field. In 1948 the archbishop of Canterbury, the most senior clergyman in Britain, recommended that the practice should be made a criminal offence. The British government did not follow that recommendation, although it did say that the practice was "undesirable and not to be encouraged."

In 1949 Italian doctor Piero Donini produced the first human fertility drug, but it took until 1962 before the first baby was born as a result of drug-induced ovulation. Meanwhile, in 1954 there was a report of four successful pregnancies following the use of frozen sperm. By this time, artificial insemination by donor was becoming increasingly popular in the United States.

Understanding Grows

As the 1960s dawned, doctors and scientists all over the world were learning more and more about different parts of the process of reproduction. All of this knowledge and understanding was needed before IVF could be developed.

Their knowledge included the use of fertility drugs to regulate the numbers of eggs that matured in the ovary. Developments in the understanding of the ways in which eggs mature and the events of ovulation were also important. As scientists moved closer toward IVF, it became vitally important that the process of fertilization was thoroughly understood. Just as vital was knowledge about the way early human embryos develop in vitro, or outside their natural environment in the body of the mother. It soon became apparent that human embryos could not survive long outside the ideal environment of the mother. It became clear that transferring an embryo back to the mother would need to be done within the first few days of fertilization.

Only once all of this knowledge and understanding was in place could scientists take the next steps forward and move toward developing IVF.

FOCUS The Early Development of the Human Embryo

How does an embryo develop? Once an egg and a sperm have joined, the two nuclei fuse together. This means that the genetic material of the father is combined with the genetic material of the mother. Once this has happened, a new cell with a unique combination of **DNA** has formed. Immediately the cell begins to divide, and about 30 hours after fertilization, the developing embryo has two cells. After 40–50 hours, each of these two cells has also divided in two, and the embryo consists of four cells. In the human body, these divisions take place as the fertilized egg is beginning to move down the fallopian tube. Cell divisions continue, until there are 16 cells. Eventually, about four to five days after fertilization, a hollow ball of around 80 cells arrives in the uterus, where it implants itself. At this stage the embryo is known as a **blastocyst**. The developing embryo in IVF can be returned to the body of the mother at any stage from two cells to blastocyst. From then on, the remaining stages of development will take place in the protected environment of the uterus.

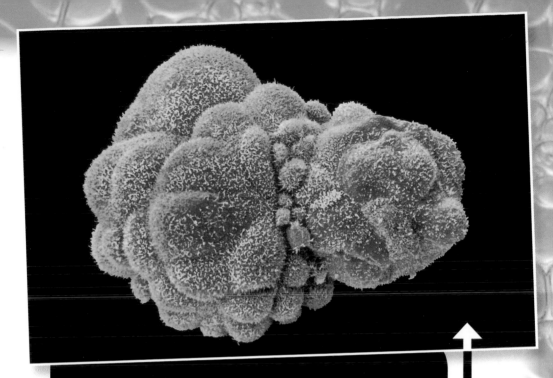

Increasingly, IVF clinics are returning the developing embryo to the uterus at the blastocyst stage, rather than at an earlier stage, because this is the point that the embryo would naturally arrive in the uterus and implant.

Enter Edwards and Steptoe

The first time a human egg was fertilized successfully outside the female body was in 1969. It was achieved by Dr. Robert Edwards, an academic **physiologist** working at Cambridge University. He used human ovaries that had been removed during surgery as the source of the eggs. The eggs needed to be kept in a special, chemically balanced fluid—they could not simply be taken out of the body and left in a dish. This first human in vitro fertilization took place in a culture medium, which is a mixture of chemicals and water used to cultivate eggs and developing embryos. The culture medium had been used successfully for the in vitro fertilization of hamster eggs during earlier, animal-based research into infertility treatments.

At the same time, Patrick Steptoe, a **gynecologist** working in the United Kingdom, was developing methods of extracting mature human eggs from the ovary by laparoscopy. He could "harvest" eggs, sucking them up from the ripe **follicle** (cell surrounding the egg) at the stage when they could be fertilized. At that time laparoscopy was considered "a dangerous procedure."

21

The Birth of IVF—and Louise Brown

By 1971 Edwards and Steptoe had met and were sharing their ideas and expertise to work toward a successful fertility treatment. They worked on retrieving eggs from volunteers so they could time egg collection to perfection. They tried to create the best culture conditions for maintaining a human egg and an early embryo outside the body—in vitro. They did not use fertility drugs to enhance egg development. They simply monitored their patients carefully, and when ovulation appeared imminent (at whatever hour of the day or night), they operated and collected the egg by laparoscopy.

Before long they felt ready to attempt a pregnancy in an infertile volunteer. By 1975 success was on the horizon—a human embryo was replaced successfully in the body of its mother, and a pregnancy began. But the excitement was short-lived. The longed-for pregnancy developed not in the uterus of the mother, but in her fallopian tube. This is known as an **ectopic pregnancy**, and it can cause terrible pain and severe damage or even death to the mother. An operation was carried out to remove the tube, and the embryo with it, destroying the hopes of doctors and scientists alike. It was also a terrible blow to the couple, who so desperately wanted a child that they were prepared to act as human guinea pigs in this amazing experiment.

Robert Edwards (on the left) and Patrick Steptoe were pioneers whose work resulted in the birth of the first IVF baby and gave hope to countless infertile couples.

However, for Edwards and Steptoe, success was not far away. They continued their experiments, in spite of growing pressure from the media and groups who were unhappy with their interference in the process of reproduction. In 1977 they removed a single mature egg from the ovary of Lesley Brown and fertilized it with sperm from her husband. The embryo that resulted was implanted back into Lesley's uterus, and to everyone's delight she became pregnant. On July 25, 1978, Louise Brown was born—a healthy baby girl conceived in a glass petri dish. This was truly groundbreaking science—and also the end of years of heartache for the Browns. Both Patrick Steptoe and Robert Edwards were present at the birth—they must have been almost as happy as Mr. and Mrs. Brown! IVF as a way of overcoming infertility had arrived at last.

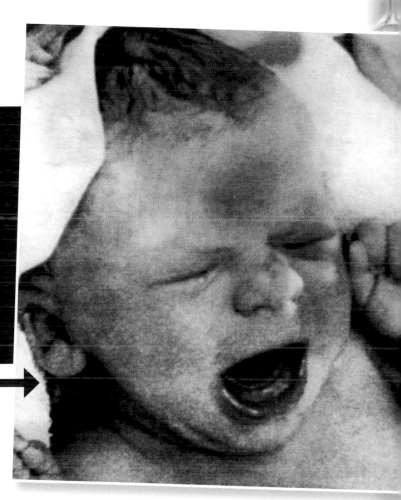

Louise Brown was the first baby born as a result of fertilization outside the body. The media coined the phrase "test-tube baby" to describe her astonishing conception, and this colloquial term for IVF stuck.

HOW DOES IVF WORK?

The birth of Louise Brown in 1978 was the climax of years of research, but it was just the beginning of new infertility treatments. In the years since then, IVF has continued to develop in a spectacular way—the techniques have been refined and new treatments have been added. Within two years, two Australian groups of researchers helped couples to have babies using IVF, but they used a different sort of technique. They gave their patients fertility drugs to make sure that plenty of eggs were produced. Because they had a higher success rate than the British team, it was their method of egg collection that became widely adopted. Even Edwards and Steptoe would have their patients use fertility drugs to stimulate the production of more than one egg, a process known as **superovulation**.

IVF offers a way to overcome infertility for women whose fallopian tubes are blocked, twisted, or damaged beyond repair, so that neither eggs nor sperm can travel along the tubes. The treatment combines the egg and sperm outside the body and returns the developing embryo to the uterus, bypassing the need for the fallopian tubes.

If a couple who are infertile because of damaged fallopian tubes decide, in consultation with their doctors, that IVF treatment is the way forward for them, what can they expect?

Starting Out

Almost every couple that undergoes IVF treatment receives initial counseling. This is to make sure that they realize that although the treatment offers them the hope of a baby, it in no way guarantees one. The chances of a couple actually achieving a successful pregnancy are no higher—and probably lower—than a fertile couple attempting to get pregnant by natural methods. If the couple do get pregnant using IVF, then the risk of a multiple pregnancy is higher than for a couple that conceives naturally. IVF clinics feel it is important that patients realize these facts before they undergo treatment.

IVF clinics vary widely in who they will accept for treatment. Couples who seek help are not just those with blocked or damaged fallopian tubes. Some couples do not get pregnant, and there is no clear reason as to why. If they have tried all other methods and failed, IVF may offer them a final chance.

Infertility clinics, such as this one in Milan, Italy, need to find out as much as they can about their patients as soon as possible, so they use medical notes from the doctors who have carried out earlier examinations into the couple's fertility problem. They also need to talk to the couple to find out what they are looking for and if they are likely to be suitable for the treatments on offer.

Age of woman	% of successful pregnancies per cycle using fresh eggs
Under 35	32.6
35–37	27.3
38–39	19.7
40–42	10.8
42+	4

Some clinics are selective about who gets treatment. For example, they may accept only younger couples who are more likely to succeed, both to avoid giving false hope to other couples and to keep their "baby per treatment" average as high as possible. The rate of live babies achieved per treatment is one of the most important factors couples look at when deciding which infertility clinic to choose.

Other clinics specialize in the most-difficult-to-treat cases, such as older couples, couples where both partners have infertility problems, and couples who have already had a number of IVF failures. Yet others are relatively unselective. This is why it is important for couples to find out as much as possible about an infertility clinic, to learn if it specializes in treatment that matches their particular problem. Figures for the number of successful pregnancies do not always tell the whole story.

The IUF Process

The first important stage of IVF treatment is to make sure that the woman produces a number of high-quality eggs. This occurs as a result of using carefully measured doses of fertility drugs. The development of ripe follicles on the surface of the ovary is then monitored. If not many follicles are developing, doctors will not try to collect eggs. Instead, they will try again during the next menstrual cycle, when they will give the woman a higher dosage of drugs.

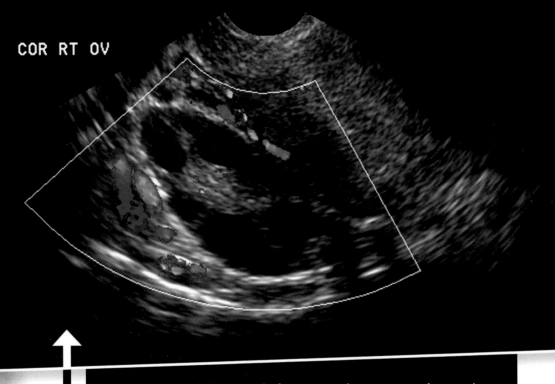

COR RT OV

This transvaginal ultrasound of a woman shows a normal appearing ovary containing numerous ovarian follicles. Colour flow dopper applied to this image shows the arterial supply to the ovary in red and the venous drainage in blue.

The development of the eggs maturing in the ovaries is monitored using **ultrasound**, which enables doctors to see how many follicles are forming. Blood tests may also be used to monitor levels of a hormone called estradiol—as the follicles develop, the level of estradiol increases. By combining the information from the blood tests and the ultrasound, doctors can build an accurate picture of how many eggs are developing in the ovary and when will be the best time to collect them. About 36 hours before the egg collection is due to occur, the woman is given an injection of another hormone, human chorionic gonadotrophin (hCG). This helps to make sure that the eggs are fully mature in their follicles.

Collecting the eggs is another vital and tense stage of the process. If a number of healthy, mature eggs are not collected, the process cannot go ahead. Ripe follicles in the ovaries do not necessarily mean that eggs will be collected successfully—harvesting eggs is a difficult and delicate procedure.

The process is carried out with the woman either sedated or under a general anesthetic. An ultrasound probe is placed inside the vagina because it gives a better picture of the position of the ripe follicles than a probe on the stomach. A needle is carefully guided through the wall of the vagina into the body cavity next to the ovaries. The point is then carefully maneuvered into a ripe follicle. The fluid inside the follicle, including the mature egg, is sucked up into a tube connected to a small jar that collects the eggs.

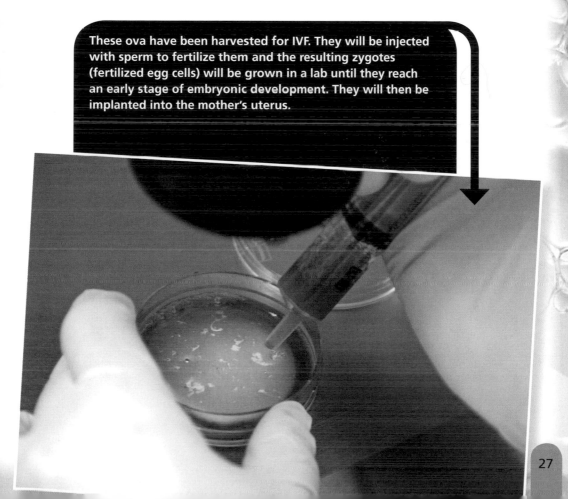

These ova have been harvested for IVF. They will be injected with sperm to fertilize them and the resulting zygotes (fertilized egg cells) will be grown in a lab until they reach an early stage of embryonic development. They will then be implanted into the mother's uterus.

The Big Moment

Once the eggs have been collected from the woman, they are placed in a special liquid that mimics normal body fluids. Each egg is put into a small dish in an incubator and kept at body temperature. The acidity level (the pH) is also kept the same as that of normal body fluids. This helps the eggs to continue to develop normally. The male partner then produces some semen, from which samples of very active sperm are taken. These are added to the dishes containing the eggs four to six hours after the eggs were collected—at the time they would naturally have been released from the ovary—and if all goes well with the insemination, the process of fertilization begins. This takes about 18 hours from start to finish, and it is then another 12 hours before the first cell division takes place. At this stage a couple will find out if any embryos have resulted.

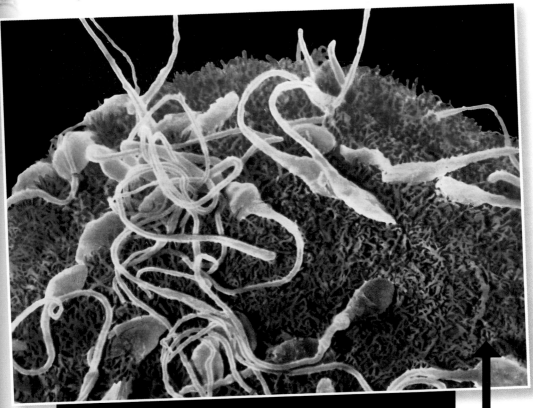

During IVF we are able to see the actual process of fertilization that would otherwise be hidden within the fallopian tubes of a woman's body. The availability of the very early embryo means it can be checked for serious genetic abnormalities before it is placed in the body of the mother.

The dividing of the embryonic cells continues for several days. After two days they contain four cells, after three days there are eight cells, and after five days the embryo is a hollow ball of cells, called a blastocyst. The embryo can be transferred to the woman's body at any of these stages. During this time the health of the tiny embryos will be monitored closely by an **embryologist**. The dividing cells are regularly observed through a microscope, and great care is taken so that only healthy, undamaged embryos are placed in the mother's body.

> *"We choose which embryos to replace by looking at their appearance. A good embryo has even cell divisions and the cells aren't forming small fragments. We have a grading system, and the best grades of embryo give the best pregnancy rates. Having said that, we sometimes have embryos with a poor appearance giving rise to healthy pregnancies and equally some beautiful embryos which don't result in pregnancy at all."*
>
> Nicola Monk, embryologist, Winterbourne Hospital Infertility Clinic

Embryo Transfer

In some ways, transferring the embryos to the mother's body is the simplest part of the IVF procedure. The hormonal state of the woman's body a few days after ovulation means that she is ready to receive an embryo. Some embryos—usually two or three—are placed in a very fine tube called a catheter, which is passed through the woman's cervix to the top of the uterus. This is the normal—and ideal—site for the embryo to implant. The tiny balls of cells are deposited in the uterus. To help improve the chances of pregnancy occurring, it is common to give a woman additional treatment using the hormone **progesterone** after the embryos have been placed in her uterus.

At this stage the woman can go home and continue with her ordinary life. Some women are tempted to simply stay in bed and not move to try to make sure that the tiny embryos remain where they are supposed to be. However, all the research shows that this does not make any difference as to whether the embryos implant or not. After all, an embryo normally implants regardless of what is going on in the life of its mother!

Finding Out

For an infertile couple, the two weeks immediately following embryo transfer might seem to be an eternity. They have to wait until the woman would be due to have a **period** before they find out if she is actually pregnant or not. Of course, if her period starts, then the IVF has obviously not worked. But if the monthly bleeding does not start on the day it is expected, then a highly sensitive early pregnancy test can show what is happening to the hormones in the body and give either good news or bad.

An ultrasound scan carried out four to six weeks after the embryos are transferred will confirm pregnancy and also give the couple their first glimpse of their longed-for child—or children! This scan provides important information to the IVF team. It shows them if they have definitely been successful and how many babies are expected. It is also enormously important for the couple concerned, who may find it difficult to accept the fact that they really are pregnant after trying for so long. Seeing a tiny blob, or blobs, on the ultrasound screen, and the beating of a tiny heart, can help to make the situation seem more real.

Not Pregnant

Pregnant

This is the sight that everyone on an IVF program longs to see. A positive pregnancy test means at least one embryo has implanted and a pregnancy has begun!

Once an IVF pregnancy has been established, it becomes just like any other pregnancy. The worries and fears that every mother has for her unborn child may well be greater in a couple who have tried for years to become pregnant, but the actual risks are no higher—unless of course the couple is expecting twins or triplets. Even then, the risks of problems developing in the pregnancy are no worse than for anyone else expecting more than one baby to arrive.

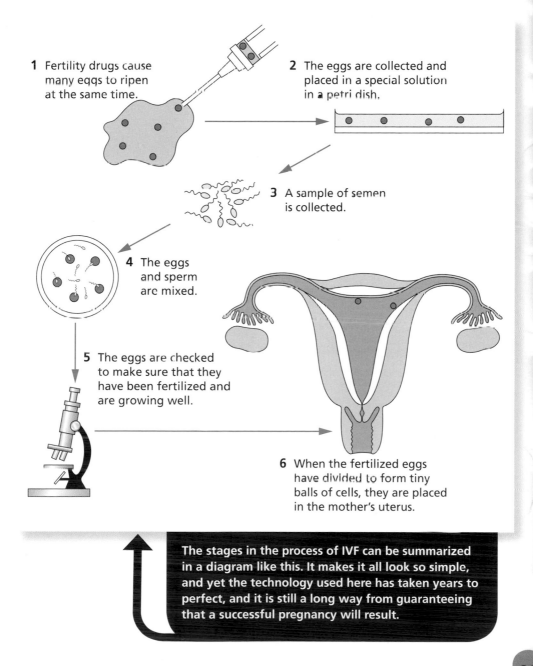

1 Fertility drugs cause many eggs to ripen at the same time.

2 The eggs are collected and placed in a special solution in a petri dish.

3 A sample of semen is collected.

4 The eggs and sperm are mixed.

5 The eggs are checked to make sure that they have been fertilized and are growing well.

6 When the fertilized eggs have divided to form tiny balls of cells, they are placed in the mother's uterus.

The stages in the process of IVF can be summarized in a diagram like this. It makes it all look so simple, and yet the technology used here has taken years to perfect, and it is still a long way from guaranteeing that a successful pregnancy will result.

THE PRICE OF SUCCESS

IVF is a technique that has improved the chances of having a baby for infertile couples all over the world. Thousands and thousands of children have been born as a result of this still relatively new technology. From an initial success rate of well below five percent, couples now have a 20–25 percent chance of pregnancy when they undergo IVF treatment. The success rate varies depending on clinical problem and the age of the woman. This success rate is similar to the chances of a fertile couple achieving a successful pregnancy if they have sexual intercourse at the woman's most fertile time of the month.

These are just some of the people that would not have been born without IVF.

The Cost of Treatment

The chances of successful IVF treatment vary greatly from clinic to clinic, and some appear far better at producing live babies from a single treatment. But what does this have to do with cost?

The cost and the way fertility treatment is paid for varies considerably from country to country. In the UK, the National Health Service (NHS) will provide one cycle of IVF treatment to infertile couples who have no children together if the woman is under 40 and has a **BMI** of 19–30. Beyond this single cycle, or if they are not eligible for treatment, people have to pay for IVF. Many other European countries provide three free cycles of treatment before couples have to pay.

In the United States, the cost averages $12,400. Currently, 15 states require that insurance companies offer fertility treatment coverage.

In Australia, the cost of a cycle of IVF is around AUS$2,500-4,000 but this is heavily subsidised by the government, so patients pay around AUS$1,000 or less per cycle. When people (or societies, in the case of the NHS) are paying out large sums of money on treatments for infertility, they have a right to know that they are getting good value for money. However, raw figures of babies born per treatment can be deceptive.

How Many Embryos?

One important factor that affects the success rate of IVF is the number of embryos transferred into the body of the woman, which varies from clinic to clinic and country to country. On the one hand, the more embryos that are transferred, the greater the chance of a successful pregnancy. On the other hand, there is a greatly increased risk of multiple pregnancies.

Multiple pregnancies—twins, triplets, or more—are known to carry a higher risk that things will go wrong. They put an immense strain on the body of the mother when she is carrying them, and they are also more difficult for parents to cope with when they are born.

If the number of embryos transferred is not carefully managed, the longed-for arrival of children to an infertile couple can put a huge strain on them, especially if they have spent much of their savings on fertility treatment. However, if clinics transferred only one embryo to reduce the risk of a multiple pregnancy, they would also reduce the likelihood of pregnancy. Questions such as these need to be weighed up carefully when couples and their doctors are deciding how to proceed with treatment.

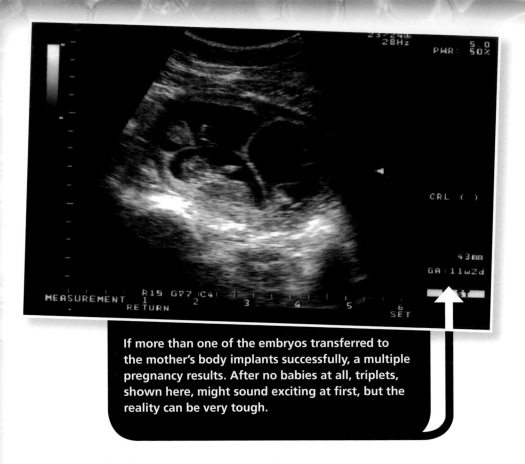

If more than one of the embryos transferred to the mother's body implants successfully, a multiple pregnancy results. After no babies at all, triplets, shown here, might sound exciting at first, but the reality can be very tough.

"In most cases, replacing more than two embryos does not increase the chance of having a baby but can substantially increase the risk of a multiple birth. There is little benefit in replacing more than two embryos and there can often be considerable physical, emotional, and financial costs."

Ruth Deech, chairperson of the Human Fertilization and Embryology Authority, or HFEA

In the United States, clinics make their own decisions about how many embroys to place in a woman's womb, but in 2006 the American Society for Reproductive Medicine and the Society for Assisted Reproductive Technology issued guidelines that no more than two embryos be transferred at one time to women under the age of 35 and that clinics should consider transferring only one. As women get older, the recommendation is that more embryos should be transferred, up to five at a time in women over 40.

In the United Kingdom, a maximum of two embryos can be implanted at any one time, to strike the best balance between giving a good chance of pregnancy with the least risk of a multiple birth. There are hopes that this will eventually be reduced to one.

In Australia, the recommendation from the Fertility Society of Australia is for two embryos to be transferred at a time, with a move to implanting just the single, best embryo in women under 40.

As techniques improve, doctors can achieve similar pregnancy rates using fewer embryos, which is better for the health and well-being of both the mother and the baby.

DISCUSS   Do Doctors Know Best?

In 2007 a team at Guy's Hospital in London led a study into a new IVF technique. They showed that growing embryos in a culture for five days (instead of the usual three) means the embryos are much more likely to implant successfully, so only one embryo would need be transferred to the mother each time. Progress such as this is welcomed by scientists and doctors, who want to cut the multiple birthrate that occurs in approximately one out of every four IVF pregnancies. Yet anxious patients, sometimes desperate to have a child, often want as many embryos as possible implanted. They are prepared to risk the problems of a multiple pregnancy in their quest to have a child.

In the United States, where people often pay for their entire treatment, multiple birth rates are particularly high. This is a dilemma for the doctors. It seems to make sense that the more embryos implanted, the better the chance of a baby. But this is not always the case, and the aim of fertility treatment is to produce a single, healthy baby. The dilemma is to convince the would-be parents that the doctors really do know best. What do you think?

DORIVER AND IAN'S STORY

Infertility involves real people. The treatments can be messy, time-consuming, and are not always successful. So what is fertility treatment really like?

Doriver and Ian Lilley got married when Doriver was 20. Six years later, they decided to start a family. But things did not go quite as planned. After 18 months, Doriver still wasn't pregnant, so the couple went to see their doctor. They were lucky—because they had already been trying for a baby for some time, and they had a sympathetic doctor, they were referred quite quickly to an infertility specialist.

None of the initial tests showed any reason why Doriver and Ian were not getting pregnant, yet nothing they tried actually worked. Even when they tried the fertility drug Clomid, nothing happened. All of the treatments that sounded so effective in theory, did not have the desired effect on the reproductive systems of Doriver and Ian.

"Every time something fails, infertility becomes harder to deal with, as you begin to realize it might not work—ever."

Doriver Lilley

When Ian and Doriver Lilley got married in 1985, they expected to spend a few years enjoying themselves and saving before settling down to family life. But things did not work out as planned…

Infertility Takes Over

For both Ian and Doriver, being completely out of control of the situation was an alien and unpleasant experience. Not conceiving made Doriver feel like she was a failure, and it was difficult having to rely on other people for such a very intimate and personal thing as having a baby. Besides, so far, even science had failed them.

By this stage their doctors felt there was little chance they would succeed in becoming pregnant. If they wanted to try IVF treatment, they would have to pay for it themselves.

Making the decision to begin IVF treatment gave Doriver and Ian a renewed sense of optimism. In their everyday life, Doriver and Ian felt the "odd ones out," the couple who could not conceive. At the IVF clinic they felt normal—everyone they met there was in the same boat. In theory, IVF should be a straightforward solution. But for many, the science and technology does not always work as it should.

"Everyone else seemed pregnant. I kept going in to work, but it was so hard to keep appearing cheerful. Every day when I got home, I'd break down and cry because I couldn't cope with it ..."

Doriver Lilley

Will IVF Be the Answer?

The first treatment was exciting. Doriver's eggs were harvested—in itself an exciting victory—and some healthy embryos were formed and transferred back into her body. They even had a weakly positive pregnancy test—but the embryos did not implant properly, the level of pregnancy hormones dropped, and the pregnancy ended just a few days later. In spite of the disappointment, Doriver was encouraged because they got eggs and they got embryos. The couple's second attempt was a crushing blow. It failed completely. Things looked bleak.

Doriver and Ian came into a small amount of money. They immediately enlisted for their third attempt at IVF. Eggs were harvested and healthy embryos formed, which were transferred into Doriver's uterus—and the waiting began. This time the pregnancy test was strongly positive—at least one embryo had definitely implanted in the uterus wall.

"I knew that statistically our chances were getting less and less each time we tried—but I also knew that as long as we had any money to spend I was going to keep on trying."

Doriver Lilley

Pregnant at Last!

At 32 years old, after six years of trying, Doriver was finally pregnant!

Six weeks passed with no problems before Doriver and Ian went for their first ultrasound scan, and when it showed two little embryos growing, they were completely overwhelmed. Not only were they pregnant, but they were expecting twins!

"There was a huge pressure to provide good quality sperm. Doriver had been through so much, everything was ready and waiting, she was in theatre and then it all hinged on my one involvement!"

Ian Lilley

After the twins were born, Doriver had little time to marvel at how they had arrived. Caring for newborn twins is enormously time-consuming and tiring—but this was what all the trying and waiting had been about. During fertility treatment, the focus is on getting pregnant—it can be easy to forget that at the end of a pregnancy there are babies that grow up into children who need to be raised.

"After embryo replacement I did everything in the house and got all our meals ready, etc. I know that you are told it doesn't make any difference [what you do in your daily life], but after so long we were not going to take that chance."

Ian Lilley

Fate had another twist, however, because just when Doriver was planning to return to work, she found she was pregnant again, without any artificial intervention. Doriver and Ian were shocked—once again the unpredictability of human fertility had thrown their carefully made plans out the window. Science has definite limitations—it had been unable to explain their infertility, and now science could not really explain their new-found fertility.

The family was thrilled when James made his entry into the world. The couple soon thought about contraception, but not before Thomas was on the way. Finally, before their fifth child, Ruthanne, was born, Doriver and Ian took steps to make sure that they would not have more children. From childlessness more than 12 years ago, Doriver and Ian are now the happy, proud, exhausted, and somewhat bemused parents of five healthy children!

Doriver and Ian with their five children. As these children grow up, there will be no way of telling that two of them would not exist if it were not for IVF technology.

BEYOND IVF

The techniques of IVF are constantly being refined and adjusted to find ways of giving the highest possible chance of success to infertile couples. For example, for many years embryos have been transferred at the four- or eight-cell stage. Recent work suggests that transferring the blastocysts (five-day-old embryos) will give better pregnancy rates, because this is the stage at which the embryo would enter the uterus during natural conception.

A number of other new technologies have been developed that help to overcome infertility problems. Most of these also involve embryo transfer.

Donor Eggs

One of the ways in which IVF has moved forward is in the use of **donor** eggs. It has been shown that if a couple are having trouble conceiving and the woman is over the age of 40, it may be necessary to use an egg donor to achieve a successful pregnancy. In these cases IVF is much more successful when the eggs of a younger woman—less than 37 years old—who is already known to be fertile herself, are used. It is not just in couples where the woman is older that donor eggs are useful. Women who have no eggs in their ovaries cannot become pregnant without an egg donor. Also, women who carry a genetic disease may need to use donor eggs to avoid passing on a debilitating illness. So the use of donor eggs in IVF and the use of donor embryos have increased the success rate for older women.

Some doctors use this technology to allow women who are much older than the natural age for childbearing to have children. Naturally, a woman passes through the menopause at between 45 and 55 years. At this point she no longer has periods, and her ovaries become inactive—no more eggs are released. But by using donor eggs or embryos, women over the age of 50 have been able to give birth.

Since the initial breakthrough in new treatments, more than 100 women aged 50 or over have had babies in the United States alone. However, only relatively few clinics will treat older women in this way. There are many people who are concerned about using the treatment on older women, both because of the potential risks to the health of the mother and the age gap between the mother and child—although similar arguments are rarely put forward when older men father children naturally!

Is Old for Women the same as Old for Men?

It is not that unusual for men to father babies in their 50s, 60s, and even 70s. Charlie Chaplin, Michael Douglas, and Paul McCartney are just a few examples of famous older fathers. If a man becomes a father when he is older, he is generally met with congratulations from those around him. If a woman becomes a mother when she is older, however, people tend to throw up their hands in horror, and the woman may be accused of being irresponsible and putting the child at risk of being an orphan. Yet statistics clearly show that men generally die sooner than women—so older dads are more likely to die and leave their children than older moms. Why is there this difference in attitudes—is it fair or right? Surely both older fathers and mothers should be congratulated on the birth of a baby, or both should be censured. Is this an area where sexism is still alive and well?

Adriana Ilieascu was 66 when she gave birth to her daughter in 2005. Artificial hormones were used to prepare her uterus, and once the pregnancy was established her body took over and maintained it as though she was a younger woman. She is not the oldest person to give birth. A Spanish woman had twins in 2006 days before her 67th birthday!

41

A Frozen Harvest

When the ovaries are encouraged to superovulate they can produce up to 12 ripe eggs in one cycle. These eggs are fertilized, and a small number of healthy embryos are then transferred back into the uterus of the mother. However, there may be other healthy embryos remaining. What should be done with them? Most IVF clinics now offer embryo freezing and storage to their clients. The early embryos are frozen and stored in flasks of liquid nitrogen.

Human sperm have been frozen and stored for years, and frozen animal embryos have been transported around the world for some time, but using frozen human embryos is recent. It seems a dramatic treatment for such delicate tissue.

This has many advantages. If the first attempt at IVF fails, the couple can have at least one, if not more, attempts without having to go through the whole process of egg collection again. If, on the other hand, the first attempt is successful, then the remaining embryos can be kept so that if the couple decide they would like another child, they have embryos ready to use. However, the presence of these frozen embryos does raise some questions. One of the simplest is—what happens to the embryos once a couple decide their family is complete?

The embryos may simply be destroyed, but this is not the most usual fate for them. If the parents are willing—and they often are—the embryos may be used for research into the treatment of human fertility. They may be allowed to continue developing until they are 14 days old, at which point further research is banned in most countries. Another alternative is that one couple may donate their "spare" embryos to another infertile couple, who cannot produce healthy embryos.

Many other couples decide to keep their frozen embryos "just in case"—although most clinics put a limit on the number of years they will keep the embryos before disposing of them. This is not a cruel gesture—no one knows for sure the effect of long-term freezing on the future health of children who might grow from the embryos.

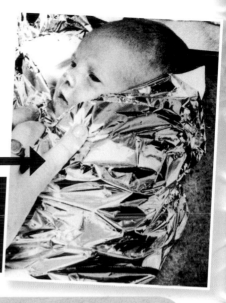

Zoe, the first baby grown from a frozen embryo, was born in Australia in 1984 and suffered no ill effects from her time in the deep freeze!

FOCUS   A Frozen Embryo Dilemma

In 2007 Natallie Evans lost her fight to be allowed to have her frozen embryos implanted. Natallie and her partner both underwent IVF treatment to create six embryos prior to Natallie receiving treatment for cancer that would make her infertile. Natallie and her partner later separated. Following the cancer treatment, Natallie's only chance of having her own biological child lay in these six embryos. By law, both parents would have to give consent for the embryos to be returned to her body. Natallie's ex-partner refused. He said he did not want to be a father and requested that the embryos be destroyed. Natallie fought the case in the European Court of Human Rights, but she was not allowed to use the embryos. Do you think this was the right decision?

"I am distraught at the court's decision. It is very hard for me to accept the embryos will be destroyed."

Natallie Evans

Life After Death?

Another scenario that must be considered is if both parents die in an accident before they have successfully had children. If there are still healthy frozen embryos, should they be implanted inside a surrogate mother and brought into the world to inherit their parents' belongings?

In all of these debates, the welfare of the potential children has to be the most important consideration. It could be extremely damaging for children to feel that they had been pawns in a divorce settlement or brought into being to make sure money stayed in the family.

In theory, frozen embryos could be kept for around 10,000 years before the natural background radiation of the Earth damaged their DNA to the extent that they would not grow and develop properly. In practice, there are often legal limits. In the United Kingdom, frozen embryos can only be kept for five years, with another five years extension possible if the parents want more time to decide if they want to add to their family. This gives a total of 10 years of embryo storage. No one knows for certain how long frozen embryos can really be stored safely, so the limit attempts to protect children who might be born damaged in some way from eggs that had been stored for longer than 10 years. Other countries have less strict laws and regulations about this. This again raises child welfare issues, making it possible for one sibling to be 30 or even 40 years younger than another. Whatever the legal situation, the existence of frozen embryos raises difficult issues.

FOCUS   Is freezing eggs a better way?

In the past, although sperm and embryos could be successfully frozen for later use, scientists could not freeze human eggs. Now it is hoped that problems like Natallie's (see page 43) will become a thing of the past as new techniques mean eggs and slices of ovarian tissue can be frozen and stored. This means women who have to undergo cancer treatment can store eggs for when they are ready to have a baby, and the choice of using the eggs will be theirs alone. However, some women want to freeze their eggs so they can concentrate on their careers when they are young and have a baby using their own eggs later in life. Is this an ethical use of the technology?

Injecting Sperm—a Major Breakthrough

Until recently there was no help for couples in which the male partner did not produce fertile sperm, apart from artificial insemination by a donor. Recent developments have changed that, and there are now techniques available that mean it is possible, in theory at least, for almost any man to father a child.

The main technique used is known as **ICSI**. This stands for Intra Cytoplasmic Sperm Injection. Eggs are harvested from a woman after treatment with fertility drugs in the same way as for IVF. A single sperm is then injected into the **cytoplasm** of each egg cell. The fertilized eggs are then observed as they divide to form early embryos. Two or three healthy embryos will then be returned to the body of the mother just as in normal IVF treatment.

> "ICSI technology has revolutionized the treatment of male factor infertility. This is considerable, because we now appreciate that male factor infertility is probably the single largest cause of infertility among couples."
>
> Dr. Simon Fischel, CARE clinic, The Park Hospital

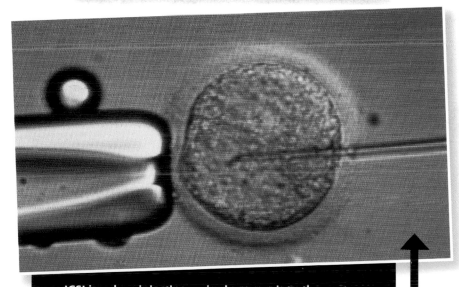

ICSI involves injecting a single sperm into the center of an egg cell so that fertilization can take place. This removes all the normal barriers to conception because the sperm cannot fail to reach the egg.

The first ICSI-produced baby was born in 1992. ICSI is now widely used and is chosen as the best treatment for at least 30 percent of all couples who undergo IVF treatment.

The steps in the ICSI procedure are shown below. This process offers two groups of patients the hope of a successful pregnancy. First, because it only takes one sperm to fertilize each egg, it helps men who have very few healthy sperm or who cannot produce semen at all. Second, it helps couples who produce healthy eggs and sperm for IVF but cannot achieve fertilization. This can be overcome by the direct insertion of a sperm into an egg.

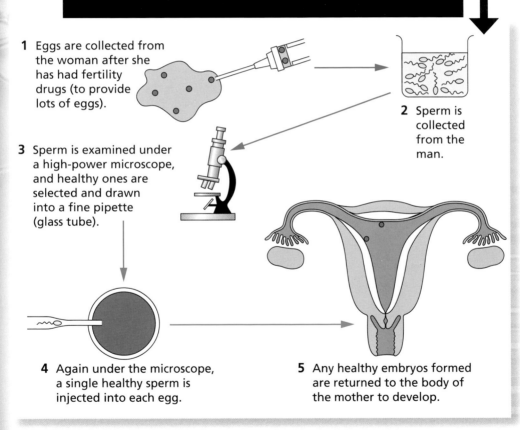

1 Eggs are collected from the woman after she has had fertility drugs (to provide lots of eggs).

2 Sperm is collected from the man.

3 Sperm is examined under a high-power microscope, and healthy ones are selected and drawn into a fine pipette (glass tube).

4 Again under the microscope, a single healthy sperm is injected into each egg.

5 Any healthy embryos formed are returned to the body of the mother to develop.

Diagnostic Testing

Another development that has followed the advances in IVF is the testing of embryos before they are transferred to the mother. There are a number of devastating diseases that result from problems in the genetic material in the nucleus of a cell. In a process known as preimplantation diagnostic testing, a single cell is removed from the early embryo (this causes it no harm). Scientists can then analyze the DNA from the cell to see if there are any genetic abnormalities. Only healthy embryos will be transferred to the mother. Some genetic diseases only affect boys, so in this case all that is needed is to identify female embryos for transfer. In other cases the testing is more specific. Parents who have already had a child affected by a severe genetic disease, such as muscular dystrophy, are now offered the chance of this early testing.

DISCUSS — Sex Selecting and Savior Siblings—Are They Acceptable?

The ability to tell the sex of an embryo before it is transferred to the uterus raises the issue of sex selection. Some people, for cultural or religious reasons, feel a need to have a son. Other couples desperately want a girl or a boy to make their family complete. Should they be allowed to pay for genetic testing and only chose embryos of the "right" sex?

Sometimes a child has a genetic illness and needs a bone marrow or umbilical cord blood transfusion to save his or her life. The donor must be the right tissue match and a brother or sister is most likely to provide it. If the parents want another child, they may request preimplantation genetic testing so that their new child is not only disease-free, but also a tissue match for their existing, ill child. These genetically selected babies are known as savior siblings. Many people find this acceptable, but others disapprove because the unwanted embryos are destroyed. What do you think?

ETHICS, ISSUES, AND THE LAW

The new reproductive technologies from IVF onward have brought great happiness to millions of couples who have been enabled to have children around the world. However, they have also raised many different issues that people as individuals and society as a whole need to consider. Some of the issues are practical and are the direct result of IVF technology.

> *"When making decisions about infertility treatment you have to consider the MEEF equation: Medical issues + Ethical issues + Emotional issues + Financial issues = Treatment."*
>
> Michael Dooley, doctor, Winterbourne Hospital Infertility Clinic

Research on embryos raises people's emotions, whether they are for or against it. While it remains legal the research will continue, and infertile couples and couples with genetic diseases will benefit from the results.

Embryo Research

The use of embryos for research is a highly sensitive issue. Without embryo research, fertility treatment would never have reached the point it is at today. Further steps forward and widening the net of people who can be helped to have a child depend on more research. Yet this research is carried out on tiny clusters of cells, some of which might, if transferred into a woman's body, turn into babies. For some people, this is difficult to accept, and there are groups of people in every country in which this type of research is carried out who strongly object to it.

Surrogate Mothers

The ability to fertilize eggs outside the body has paved the way for another controversial form of fertility treatment—the use of a **surrogate mother**. Some women have ovaries that work just fine, but they do not have a uterus, while some women have no reproductive organs at all. Their only chance of having a baby, apart from adoption, is if another woman will carry a fetus for them. This might involve IVF, with embryos from one couple transferred into the uterus of another woman, or it might involve artificial insemination of the surrogate mother with sperm from the father. Whatever the method, the baby grows and develops inside the surrogate mother, who then hands the baby over to its parents very shortly after birth.

There are all kinds of problems with surrogacy. In some countries it is legal, but there can be no payment given to a woman for carrying another person's child. In the United States, it is legal and is carried out for money by a number of very successful businesses. The biggest problem is if the surrogate mother decides she cannot hand over the child. There have been legal battles between biological and surrogate parents. In the first test case in the United States, the "purchasing" parents were granted custody of the child, while the surrogate mother was granted visiting rights.

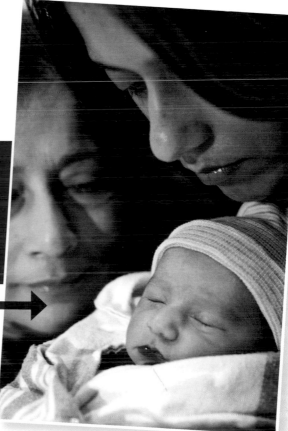

At 54, Rebecca Tejwani (left), lovingly volunteered to be a surrogate mother for her daughter Sapna Signh (right). They are seen here with newborn Syrus Sunny.

The Law

With the arrival of new technologies there have been legal problems. When dealing with potential human life the risks are great, and different countries have are dealing with them in different ways. The first concern in most legislation is the welfare of any potential children born using new technology. If there is concern that the health or well-being of the babies conceived might be affected by the technology, then most countries are unhappy about its use.

IVF began in the United Kingdom, and it responded to this giant step forward with a regulatory body known as the Human Fertilization and Embryology Authority, or HFEA. Set up in 1991, the HFEA makes sure that all clinics offering IVF and other fertility treatments in the United Kingdom meet strict standards. It collects information about success

When people wish to change the law they often stage a protest, like these people here. Attempts to change national law in Australia to allow states to ban IVF for single people sparked off such protests.

rates and provides information to the public. The HFEA also licenses and monitors all embryo research, supervising what is going on and balancing what should and should not be done. Decisions are made by the 21 members of the authority, who are experts in relevant fields. To make sure that a wide spectrum of views are heard, more than half of the team are not involved in medicine or human embryo research. In the United Kingdom, things are relatively straightforward. If a treatment is allowed by the HFEA it goes ahead; if it is not, it doesn't.

There is no national legislation in Australia on fertility treatment. However, individual states vary in that some have legislation and others do not. For example, Victoria wanted to prevent single people from receiving IVF treatment. This caused an uproar in the gay community, because two people of the same sex cannot legally marry in Australia. This means that any lesbian woman wanting to have a child is classified as single, so she would not be allowed to have fertility treatment. In response to the outcry commonwealth law was used to stop the state law in 2000.

> "The first IVF baby was born in the UK and we were the first statutory government body to regulate this treatment and remain one of the few to do so. While the number of couples seeking IVF treatment rapidly increases we aim to assure a high standard of care and medical expertise whether that clinic is private or public, big or small."
>
> Ruth Deech, HFEA chairperson

In the United States there is a similarly fragmented situation. There are few laws controlling which techniques or research may or may not be carried out. However, legislation compelling medical insurance companies to pay for IVF treatment is being introduced in an increasing number of states, making IVF and other treatments available to more and more couples. Evidence shows that in states with legislation in place that requires insurance companies to offer IVF treatment, the number of high-risk, multiple pregnancies as a result of treatment is much lower than in states where people have to pay for themselves. Naturally, when people desperately want children, but have limited funds, they will request as many embryos as possible be transferred to try to reduce the number of treatment cycles needed. With no national legislation to limit embryo numbers, some doctors will go with the patients' wishes rather than recognized best practice. But this carries risks for both mothers and babies. There are campaigns in the United States to try to ensure that all states have legislation for insurers to cover fertility treatment.

A Matter of Faith

The decisions a couple make about fertility treatments may be affected by their religious beliefs. There is no single view within the different faiths about fertility treatments such as IVF. This means that one couple may undergo IVF certain in the belief that it is acceptable, while another couple, equally desperate to have a child, may feel unable to accept IVF.

Below are summaries of the official views of some major religions, regarding infertility treatments and related issues. It is important to remember, however, that many people who consider themselves followers of a certain religion may not necessarily agree with the strict, official view handed down by their faith's leaders. In fact, within some faiths there may be disagreement among religious leaders about what is and is not acceptable. In addition to religious beliefs, couples often need to think about the effect infertility is having on their mental and physical health and seek medical as well as religious advice before making a decision.

THE CATHOLIC STANDPOINT

The teaching of the Catholic Church on fertility treatments is strict and is the same in every country. In 1987 the Pope made the Catholic position very clear in a document called *Donum vitae* ("Respect for life"). He said that treatments such as IVF are not acceptable because they separate the conception of a child from the sexual act between the parents. The Catholic Church also rejects completely any fertility treatment that involves donated eggs, sperm, or embryos as gravely immoral because of the introduction of another person into the marriage bond.

A MUSLIM PERSPECTIVE

Within Islam the production of children is a vitally important part of married life. Islamic teaching also states that for every illness, there is a cure, so it is regarded as acceptable and right that an infertile couple seek help. Treatments such as fertility drugs and procedures to open up the fallopian tubes are generally acceptable. Islamic scholars also accept the use of IVF, but only if enormous care is taken that only the eggs and sperm of the husband and wife concerned are used in the treatment. But, as in many other religions, the use of donated eggs, sperm, or embryos is seen as completely unacceptable because it breaks the unity of the marriage bond.

The spiritual dimension of many people's lives—their religion—is important in guiding their decisions about fertility treatments.

THE JEWISH APPROACH

As in so many other religions, the family is very important to the Jewish faith. Orthodox Jewish law finds assisted reproduction acceptable in helping a Jewish couple to conceive a child as long as the eggs and sperm come from the parents themselves. IVF using sex cells from the parents is acceptable, and there is often a **rabbinic** supervisor present to make sure that the eggs and sperm are not contaminated by material from non-Jews. But the use of donor eggs or sperm is much less acceptable, and certainly not allowed if the sex cells are not from Jewish people.

THE HINDU APPROACH

For Hindus, with their beliefs in reincarnation and caste (inherited social status), treatments such as IVF raise many problems. Only a husband is allowed to touch his wife, so a doctor cannot intervene in the act of conception, and fear of caste contamination makes donor eggs and sperm unacceptable to strict Hindus.

WHERE DO WE GO FROM HERE?

Some of the most exciting but controversial developments in bioscience and medicine at the moment come as offshoots of IVF treatments. They include cloning, **genetic engineering**, and **stem cell** research.

Cloning ...

Cloning mammals involves making an identical copy of an adult animal. The nucleus of an adult cell is placed in an empty egg cell. The early embryo that develops is transferred to a surrogate mother to develop. Cloning has been successful in animals such sheep, cats, horses, and even monkeys.

People are now wondering if and when the cloning of humans will take place. IVF would make it possible, because the cloned cell would have to be transferred to a uterus to develop into a baby. However, many people are suspicious: will rich and famous people try to clone themselves to become immortal, or will another Adolf Hitler try to use such technology along with genetic engineering to produce a "master race" of people? In some countries it is illegal to attempt to clone a human being, but in others some scientists are already planning to try to produce the first human clone. They feel it will help to overcome the problem of infertility—if an infertile woman can give birth to a clone of her partner or herself, it would remove the need to use donor sperm or eggs, which can be in short supply and cause religious problems.

This foal, born in 2005, is the first horse clone. It was cloned from Pieraz, winner of two endurance world championships, by an Italian company in an attempt to preserve the genetic heritage of the champion.

... and Genetic Engineering

Scientists can change the genetic material of an organism in a process known as genetic engineering (or genetic modification). This has been done successfully in many organisms, from bacteria to mice and sheep. Now scientists are trying to replace faulty genes in people affected by genetic diseases with healthy genes, with little success so far. However, the most exciting and most challenging possibility is to change the DNA of an embryo formed outside the body. If faulty genes can be replaced with healthy ones before the embryo is transferred to the mother, all the cells of the baby would contain healthy DNA. The genetic disease would be cured and no longer passed on. But this raises huge ethical questions. If the genes can be changed to cure disease, would some people want to engineer their embryos to be intelligent, tall, or beautiful? It is certain that one day it will be possible to genetically engineer human embryos—but will it ever be acceptable?

Down syndrome is one of many inherited genetic disorders. For some families, genetic screening and IVF offer ways of ensuring that their children are free from the disease. However, some couples feel they cannot use these methods because it is against their faith.

Spin-Off Technology

In 1998, in a breakthrough that caused ripples of excitement through the scientific and medical world, two American scientists cultured human embryonic stem cells that were still capable of forming almost all cell types. One team took their cells from spare embryos that had been produced during IVF fertility treatments and donated by the parents for scientific research, rather than being destroyed. The other team took human embryonic stem cells from fetuses that had been aborted at 5–9 weeks of gestation.

There was enormous excitement in the scientific world about this breakthrough. In theory at least, these embryonic cells could be encouraged to grow into almost any different type of cell needed in the body. This raised the hope of cures for diseases such as Parkinson's and Alzheimer's, the repair of spinal injuries, new heart muscle cells to repair hearts damaged by heart attacks, and new and effective treatments for strokes, burns, and arthritis. Scientists even hope that embryo stem cells might eventually be used to grow whole new organs for people waiting desperately for a transplant.

At the moment no one is sure just how the cells in an embryo are switched on or off to form particular types of tissue—kidney rather than liver, or liver rather than heart. As the answers to these questions are found, the potential will be there for a limitless supply of new organs. Not only that, but the problem of rejection of tranferred organs could be solved. The immune system does not attack and destroy a developing embryo, even though it has different **antigens** on its cells to its mother. New organs created from embryo stem cells may have this protection.

DISCUSS   The Ethical Problem

The major ethical problem with research using embryonic stem cells is that they come from spare embryos used in fertility treatments. Many people, including many religious groups, feel that it is wrong to use a potential human being as a source of material in this way. It is also argued that the embryo cannot give permission, so using it is a violation of its human rights. In the United Kingdom, there was considerable debate before legislation was passed to extend the Human Fertilization and Embryology Act, which allows embryonic stem cell research to take place. State funding for research into embryonic stem cells was blocked in the United States. After considerable debate the government decided that from August 2001, such work could continue on the cells as long as rigid criteria were observed.

The use of embryonic stem cells from the umbilical cord of newborn babies may help to overcome some of the reservations. It may become possible to store stem cells from every newborn baby ready for when they might need them later in their lives. Scientists are also finding stem cells in adults that appear to have the ability to grow into several different types of tissue. There seem to be more limitations with adult stem cells than with embryonic ones, but this is another possible way forward, which could avoid both rejection problems and the controversial use of embryonic tissue. Most recently scientists have found a way of reprogramming adult skin cells that makes them revert to stem cells. Again this removes many ethical issues, but raises some major scientific stumbling blocks.

Into the Future

The future of fertility treatments looks bright. The techniques are being refined and improved all the time, and the numbers of people who have a child through IVF or related treatments continue to grow. Hundreds of thousands of IVF babies are alive today, children who would not exist without the miracle of groundbreaking scientific techniques that allow eggs to be fertilized outside their mother's body. The benefits to the individuals concerned are immeasurable, and society also benefits from the birth of more children free from genetic diseases.

However, there are two sides to every story, and many people are questioning the acceptability of some of the treatments now being suggested, such as cloning and the use of spare embryos for the development of medical treatments. However, the clock cannot be turned back: we cannot return to the situation before these treatments were discovered, nor would most people wish to do so. The development of IVF and other treatments will continue for the foreseeable future, fulfilling the growing demand, and the debate within society will continue alongside it.

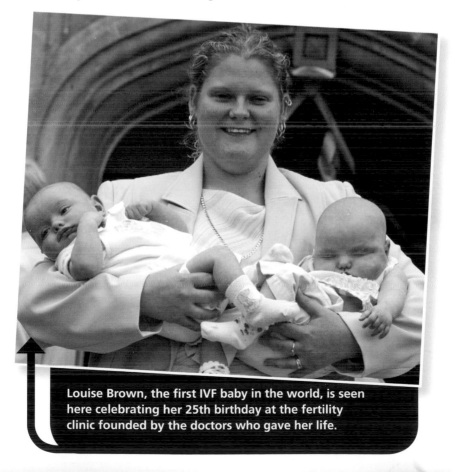

Louise Brown, the first IVF baby in the world, is seen here celebrating her 25th birthday at the fertility clinic founded by the doctors who gave her life.

TIMELINE

200 CE

Records show Jewish thinkers discussed the possibility of accidental or unintentional artificial insemination.

1954

Four successful pregnancies take place using previously frozen sperm.

1949

Dr. Piero Donini, an Italian, produces the first human fertility drug.

1945

Early reports of artificial insemination using donor sperm are published in the *British Medical Journal.*

1960s

A rapid increase in understanding of the female reproductive system and the process of fertilization occurs. Drugs are developed that stimulate ovaries so they produce eggs, and laparoscopy methods are improved, making the treatment safer.

1962

First baby is born as a result of drug-induced ovulation.

1969

Human fertilization in vitro is achieved for the first time.

2001

Teams in the United States and Italy announce that they are working on producing the first human clone.

A 62-year-old French woman who wants a child to inherit her property and money has a baby through IVF, using sperm from her brother and a donated egg.

1998

Growing embryonic stem cells in a laboratory opens the way for different types of cells and organs to be grown when they are needed for use in transplant surgery. Some of these stem cells come from "spare" embryos donated by a couple who have had successful IVF treatment.

2004

All infertile couples in the United Kingdom that meet criteria of age and body mass index are entitled to one free cycle of IVF treatment.

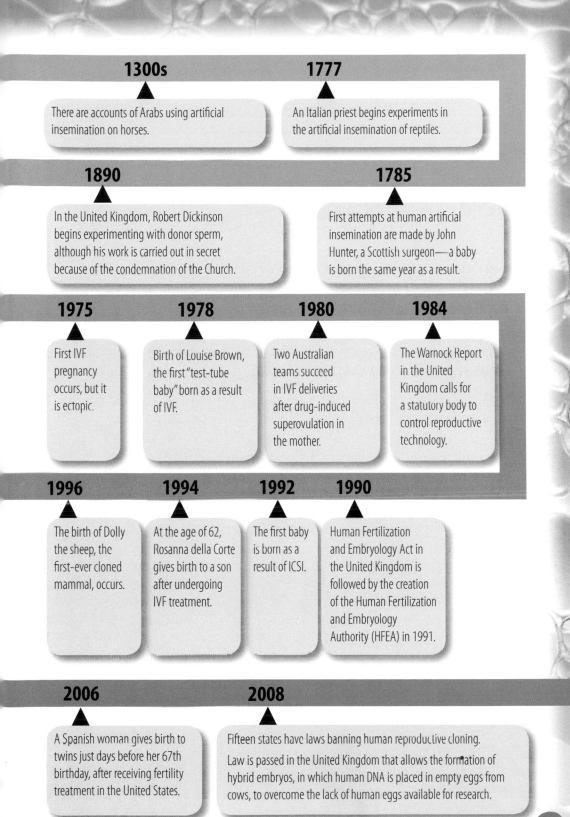

1300s

There are accounts of Arabs using artificial insemination on horses.

1777

An Italian priest begins experiments in the artificial insemination of reptiles.

1890

In the United Kingdom, Robert Dickinson begins experimenting with donor sperm, although his work is carried out in secret because of the condemnation of the Church.

1785

First attempts at human artificial insemination are made by John Hunter, a Scottish surgeon—a baby is born the same year as a result.

1975

First IVF pregnancy occurs, but it is ectopic.

1978

Birth of Louise Brown, the first "test-tube baby" born as a result of IVF.

1980

Two Australian teams succeed in IVF deliveries after drug-induced superovulation in the mother.

1984

The Warnock Report in the United Kingdom calls for a statutory body to control reproductive technology.

1996

The birth of Dolly the sheep, the first-ever cloned mammal, occurs.

1994

At the age of 62, Rosanna della Corte gives birth to a son after undergoing IVF treatment.

1992

The first baby is born as a result of ICSI.

1990

Human Fertilization and Embryology Act in the United Kingdom is followed by the creation of the Human Fertilization and Embryology Authority (HFEA) in 1991.

2006

A Spanish woman gives birth to twins just days before her 67th birthday, after receiving fertility treatment in the United States.

2008

Fifteen states have laws banning human reproductive cloning.

Law is passed in the United Kingdom that allows the formation of hybrid embryos, in which human DNA is placed in empty eggs from cows, to overcome the lack of human eggs available for research.

GLOSSARY

antigen special marker molecule sticking out from the surface of cell membranes (outer covering of cell)

artificial insemination inserting sperm into the vagina using a device, rather than through sexual intercourse

blastocyst hollow ball of cells formed after the fertilization of an egg

BMI (Body Mass Index) measure of body fat based on height and weight

cervix lower part of the uterus that extends into the vagina

conception fertilization of an egg by a sperm, followed by the egg's implantation in the wall of the uterus

contraception using a condom, contraceptive pill, or other method to prevent the conception of a baby

cytoplasm jellylike substance that fills the cell and in which the components of the cell are suspended

DNA (deoxyribonucleic acid) type of nucleic acid found in the nucleus of a cell, which carries the genetic code

donor someone who gives an organ or a product of their body—for example, eggs or sperm—to help someone who has a faulty organ or product

ectopic pregnancy pregnancy in which the embryo implants and develops in one of the fallopian tubes instead of in the uterus

embryo term for an egg after it has been fertilized, when it is in its early stages of development

embryologist doctor or scientist who specializes in the study of embryos

enzyme special protein that makes possible or speeds up the rate of chemical reactions

estrogen female sex hormone made by the ovaries, involved in the release of a mature egg

ethics consideration of what is morally right or wrong

fallopian tube one of a pair of tubes that link the ovaries and the uterus in the female reproductive system

fertility, fertile ability to produce offspring

fertility drugs chemicals that stimulate the development of mature eggs in the follicles of the ovary

fertilization union of an egg and sperm that is necessary to produce offspring

follicle cell surrounding a developing egg in the ovary

Follicle Stimulating Hormone (FSH) sex hormone that causes some of the follicles of the ovary to ripen and the eggs within them to mature

genetic to do with the genes, the units of inheritance that are passed from parent to offspring and that determine the offspring's characteristics. Each gene is made from a length of DNA, which is found in the nucleus of a cell.

genetic engineering process by which the genetic material of a cell may be altered either by replacing damaged genetic material or adding extra genetic material

gynecologist doctor who specializes in problems of the female reproductive system

hormone chemical messenger made in one place in the body which has an effect somewhere else in the body

ICSI Intra Cytoplasmic Sperm Injection, the injection of a single sperm directly into the cytoplasm of an egg cell

in vitro term meaning "in glass" in Latin, used to describe the fertilization of an egg in a petri dish

infertility, infertile inability to produce offspring

laparoscopy technique for looking at the fallopian tubes by inserting an instrument into the abdomen

menstrual cycle approximate 28-day cycle of female fertility

mucus slimy substance produced by membranes in some parts of the body

nucleus (plural **nuclei**) central part of a cell, which controls many cell functions and contains a person's DNA

ovaries pair of female sex organs where eggs mature and are stored and where the sex hormones estrogen and progesterone are produced

ovulation release of a mature egg from the ovary

ovum (also known as the egg) female sex cell

period time (5–7 days), known as menstruation, in the middle of the menstrual cycle when pregnancy has not occurred that the lining of the uterus is shed, resulting in bleeding

petri dish small, shallow dish made from thin glass, traditionally used for studying the behavior of bacteria

physiologist someone who studies the human body and its functions

pituitary gland small structure in the brain that produces many hormones

progesterone hormone of pregnancy that prevents menstruation from occurring

puberty stage when the body of a child undergoes physical development to become a sexually mature adult

rabbinic concerned with Jewish law

reproduction making of a new individual

semen mixture of sperm and fluids produced by a man when he ejaculates (discharges semen)

sperm male sex cell

statutory having legal authority

stem cell "immortal" cell that retains the ability to divide and multiply and to create other types of cell. Stem cells are found in embryos, bone marrow, skin, intestine, and muscle tissue.

superovulate when women produce many mature follicles containing mature eggs ready for release at the same time

surrogate mother woman who carries a baby for a couple who are unable to have a child of their own

testes pair of male sex organs in which sperm and semen are produced, along with the male sex hormone testosterone

ultrasound using extremely high frequency sound waves to produce images of inside the human body. Ultrasound is used for examining developing babies in the uterus.

uterus organ of the female reproductive system in which the baby grows and develops (also known as the womb)

FIND OUT MORE

Further Reading

Fullick, Ann. *Why Science Matters: Pregnancy and Birth*. Chicago: Heinemann Library, 2009.

Parker, Steve. *In Vitro Fertilization.* Milwaukee: World Almanac Library, 2007.

Wilson, Michael R. *Fertility.* New York: Rosen Publishing Group, 2009.

Websites

The following websites give information on different types of infertility treatment, the history of reproductive medicine, and finding the right fertility treatment:

www.hfea.gov.uk
This website of the Human Fertilization and Embryology Authority in the United Kingdom explores infertility, treatments, and issues related to fertility treatment and research.

www.pbs.org/wgbh/amex/babies/
Learn about and watch a one-hour documentary called *Test Tube Babies*, which tells the story of doctors, researchers, and couples first involved in IVF treatment. You can also learn more about the ethical questions presented by IVF and watch couples who have been through IVF talk about their experiences.

www.resolve.org
Website for the infertility association, Resolve, which offers advice, information, and resources for couples who are having difficulty conceiving.

INDEX

artificial insemination 19, 45, 49, 52

blastocysts 20, 21, 29, 40
Brown, Louise 23, 57

cervix 8, 14, 29
child welfare issues 44, 50
cloning 54
conception 8–9, 13, 40, 52
contraception 4, 11
counseling 24

DNA 20, 44, 47, 55
dye tests 14

ectopic pregnancy 22
Edwards, Dr. Robert 21, 22, 23, 24
eggs (ova) 4, 5, 6, 7, 8, 9, 12–13, 16, 17, 20, 21, 24, 26–28
    donor eggs 13, 40, 52, 53, 54
    fertilization 4, 5, 9, 13, 15, 18, 20, 21, 28, 42, 45, 49, 57
    frozen 33, 44
    harvesting 21, 22, 27, 37, 45, 46
embryos 5, 20, 22, 24, 28–29, 45
    donor embryos 40, 52, 53
    embryo research 35, 48, 51, 56
    embryonic stem cells 55–56
    frozen 33, 42–43, 44

genetic modification 55
implantation 9, 20, 21, 29, 30, 34, 35, 37
preimplantation diagnostic testing 47
transfer 29, 33, 34, 35, 40, 51
estrogen 7
ethical issues 5, 48–53, 56

fallopian tubes 7, 8, 9, 13–14, 14, 20, 22, 24, 52
fertility 6, 10, 11, 15, 18, 42
fertility drugs 16, 17, 19, 20, 24, 26, 36, 45, 52
Follicle Stimulating Hormone (FSH) 7, 13, 17
follicles 21, 26, 27

genetic diseases 15, 28, 40, 47, 55, 57
genetic engineering 54, 55
genetics 9, 20

hormones 6–7, 13, 17, 19, 26, 27, 29
Human Fertilization and Embryology Authority (HFEA) 34, 50, 51
hysterosalpingogram 13, 14

ICSI (Intra Cytoplasmic Sperm Injection) 45, 46

in vitro fertilization (IVF) 5, 11, 16, 18–35
    background to 18–20
    case history 36–39
    ethical issues 48–53, 56
    failed treatments 30, 37, 42
    first instance of 21
    process 24–31
    success rates 25, 32
infertility 5, 10–15, 18, 37, 54
    funding treatment 3, 37, 51
    lifestyle factors 10, 14, 16
    physical and chemical causes 11–14
infertility clinics 25, 33, 34–5, 50, 51

laparoscopy 14, 21, 22
legal issues 49, 50–51

menstrual cycle 6, 8, 16, 26
menstruation 7
multiple pregnancies 4, 17, 24, 31, 33, 35, 51

older women 35, 40–41
ovaries 6, 7, 12, 16, 17, 19, 21, 26, 40, 49

ovulation 7, 8, 12, 13, 16, 19, 20, 22, 29
    superovulation 24, 42

periods 30, 40
pituitary gland 7, 19
pregnancy tests 30, 37
progesterone 29
religious issues 52–53
reproduction 6–9, 18, 20

semen 7, 8, 14, 28
sex selection 47
sperm 4, 5, 7, 8–9, 13, 14, 15, 24, 28, 38
    abnormal 15, 16
    donor sperm 15, 19, 52, 53, 54
    frozen 19, 42, 44
    injecting 5, 15, 45, 46
    sperm count 14, 15
Steptoe, Patrick 21, 22, 23, 24
surrogate mothers 44, 49, 54

"test-tube babies" 23
testes 7, 14, 19

ultrasound scans 26, 30, 38
uterus 7, 8, 9, 13, 17, 20, 21, 24, 29, 40, 49